THE 10 PRINCIPLES

TO BECOMING

A SUCCESSFUL

NURSE

CHRISTINE N. MALONE MSN, RN

The opinions expressed in this manuscript are solely the opinions of the author. The author has represented and warranted full ownership and or legal rights to publish all the materials in this book.

10 KEYS TO BECOME A SUCCESSFUL NURSE

All Rights Reserved.

Copyright 2018 Christine N. Malone

This book may not be reproduced, transmitted, or stored in whole or in any part by any means, including graphic, electronic, or mechanical without the express written consent of the publisher except in the case of brief quotations embodied in critical articles and reviews.

HarmonyLives Publishing Co.

http://www.harmonylives.com

ISBN: 978-0-578-20421-5

Printed in the United States of America

CONTENTS

Introduction

1. Am I Nursing Material?   9
2. Why Do I Want To Be A Nurse?   17
3. What Is The Nursing Discipline?   25
4. How To Prepare Myself To Become A Nurse?   32
5. How To Study For Exams and Pass?   39
6. How To Approach My Instructors?   47
7. How To Deal With Fear of Failure?   53
8. What Does A Good Nurse Look Like?   61
9. What Are The Rewards Of A Nursing Career?   72
10. How Do I Invest In A Nursing Career?   78

¨INTRODUCTION¨

Nursing is not just a job, it is my calling. It is my ministry. At the same time it is amongst many opportunities to help people through some of the happiest and worst moments. Nursing has been one of the most rewarding careers anyone always striving to make an impact on the lives of others. Dedication and commitment are two essential principles applied every day of my nursing career. Nurses are the lifeblood of the healthcare system providing and assisting the healthcare team to promote healing. Nursing is a unique profession with the ability to enhance lives and encourage wellness witnessing miracles in life and miracles in death.

Throughout my career I am thankful for all the support from the people who helped me along the way; whether from family members instructors or nurse managers. To the ones who planted the seed of a warrior when on the battlefield to never give up no matter what. Also the strong everlasting friendships built with hundreds of nurses I've worked with over the years. The emotional connections with nurses who became like family creating lasting memories. Then there are the memories spent with patients and family members with the opportunity to bless countless lives.

The rewards of my nursing career are numerous with so many amazing highlights. Nursing has provided for me so many opportunities to broaden my horizon in education and clinical skills. This book is written to motivate, encourage and aspire younger generations of nurses to gravitate to the nursing discipline.

Born the oldest of three children was always taking care of my siblings. In Junior High I began taking a course in Pre-Health and from that point a desire start brewing in my spirit to become a nurse. At the time feelings of self doubt and low self-esteem engulfed me believing this could never come true for a young girl coming from a poor family. This was only a dream. In my first book, Addiction Through The Eyes of a Nurse, Rising Above Adversity Through Faith, my story share my story of hard times, perseverance and trusting in God, becoming a nurse only by His grace. Realizing much later in my career nursing is truly my calling from God. Today I still love nursing today as much as when I began first 28 years ago

Nursing has become one of the fastest growing careers in the healthcare industry. In nursing school you will be equipped with tools to care and respond to the sick using your critical thinking skills trained by qualified PhD and Master degree nursing staff. You will be prepared to assess a patient's condition to ensure the best possible care is given. Courses will be introduced that are required for professional learning. The clinical hands on experience will help you gain insight into what nurses actually do. You will be able to integrate professional learning experiences when you become a professional nurse.

After completing nursing school you will know which specialty you want to pursue. Nursing careers are often challenging but many nurses find caring for patients so rewarding. There are several levels of nursing and can be confusing. The Licensed Practical Nurse attain a certificate and Registered Nurse attain through a professional nursing degree; Associate's,

Bachelor's, Masters or PHD according to the number of years required in school.

LPN common duties consist of data collection, assists with administering medications, monitor vital signs, monitor catheters and drains, dress wounds and assist with bathing and dressing. RN common duties consist of recording medical histories, performing diagnostic test, assessment of patient/family overall needs, intravenous pushes of medications, treatments, charging in leadership roles and delegating assignments.

Many RN's who start with a Diploma or Associate's Degree in Nursing, go on to earn their Bachelor' Degree (BSN) to qualify for management positions. Those who desire to go into advanced practice can earn a Master's and Doctorate Degree.

CHAPTER 1

AM I NURSING MATERIAL?

Nursing isn't for everyone. It takes a special person who is caring and has a passion for people. Nursing is more than just a job and you need more than an education or nursing license to be good at it. If you are considering a nursing career, first make sure that you have what it takes. Since it is a nurse's job to provide patient care, you need to be caring. Caring consist of commitment, conscience, competence, compassion and confidence consistently applied in the workplace. Commitment means you are continually dedicated to putting your best foot forward. You go above and beyond expected behavior and uphold strong values. Conscience means you have a strong sense of moral responsibility and guidance of actions even when stress challenges the application of best nursing care. You work consistently on another's behalf. Competence is arriving to work and presenting yourself in a professional manner. You hold yourself to high standards when fulfilling duties. Compassion is being empathetic with your patients and provide kind and considerate treatment at all times. Confidence is shown in your personal skills, knowledge, experiences and education. You always perform at high level while helping patients and families deal with difficult news. You have a strong sense of self invoking a positive change in patient care.

You must be able to convey kindness toward patients, even if they are demanding, confused, aggressive or rude. Although kindness and compassion is synonymous both are qualities no longer notable in society. Kindness is simply caring for your patient and being present offering companionship. It means paying attention to others, conveying openness and generosity. A nurse must be sympathetic, understanding the pain or diagnosis patients are going through in order to provide comfort. While you need to know when to tune into your patient's emotional state, you also need to know when to distance yourself. You need to remain emotionally stable during times of human suffering, emergencies, and challenging medical situations is a necessary quality. Being a nurse is stressful and every day you are faced with traumatic events that require quick critical thinking skills. You will encounter many life-saving surgeries to unexpected deaths. Remaining calm and thinking clearly under such circumstances is vital to being able to carry out the responsibilities of this position.

You must be able to communicate well is of upmost importance, because you will spend most of your time in close contact with your patients, families and doctors. You will need to be able to make sure that patients understand their complicated conditions. You also need to possess good listening skills, being attentive to what your patients say directly, as well as what they may not. Open and honest communication with both patient and their families is extremely important so they are able to clearly understand procedures and treatments. Nurses have to clearly communicate with doctors about patients and make sure they themselves understand any instructions they are given.

Nurses treat patients in both minor and serious conditions and must accept responsibility in both. They are responsible for assessing patient conditions, providing the proper treatment, and determining when further consultation is necessary. Nurses also **have to be extremely detail** oriented as they need to be able to keep track of minor changes in their patients' health or behavior, and correctly record it. When it comes to a patient's condition, neglecting to notice something could end up having serious consequences. Nurses must also accept the responsibility of their job's time demands and must be flexible and adaptive. The job of a nurse is usually not set to specific hours or schedules. With emergencies occurring at any time, nurses are often required to work overtime, nights, weekends, and holidays.

Ask yourself if you are, self motivated and goal oriented, calm and collected, emphatic and understanding, caring and kind hearted and optimistic and confident? Do you thrive in a fast paced environment, enjoy spending your work day surrounded by people, effectively manage change and adapt quickly, work well with a diverse team, and desire a job with high autonomy? If this description fits you then you have what it takes to become a successful nurse.

It would be great if you never had to encounter a difficult decision or confront controversy in the healthcare field. Unfortunately the nursing profession is not immune to these kinds of situations and you will need to make difficult choices when it comes to the patients wellness. In the Code of Ethics for Nurses will help you choose the right thing to do when it isn't always obvious. It provides direction and assistance in a profession where tough decisions will inevitably be made. Your professional nursing ethics prepare you to be the best in your career. In all your relationships practice with compassion and respect for every patient unrestricted by considerations of social or economic status, personal attributes or health problems. Your primary concern should be for the patient and their wishes should be honored. You should promote, advocate and protect the patients rights, safety and health.

One very important tool in the nursing profession is excellent communication skills. Communication is a continuous process and extremely important for all who are involved. Nurse to nurse report which occurs at the end of each shift is a fundamental part of the nursing profession can result in effective care or ineffective care caused by lack of communication. In the nursing profession, you will be responsible for persons who are ill and rely on you to be their advocate. Poor communication skills has been linked to preventable medication errors and injuries to the patients.

Learning to be a nurse with good communication skills in both a personal and professional settings, may reduce stress, promote wellness and improve overall quality of life. In today's society you will be speaking to various educational, cultural and social backgrounds and must communicate in an effective caring manner. Speak slowly and carefully pronouncing each word because certain words sound similar to one another. Speak clearly, not loud especially when speaking to elderly patients. Your inclination might be to speak loud to make them understand. Avoid any slang because this is not appropriate for a professional. Stop and listen to what your patient is saying to you. Listening is a powerful tool.

In the Nightingale era, uniforms enhanced the image, pride, and work of nurses. The uniforms differentiated nurses from servants, cooks and laundresses. Civil War soldiers recognized the authority of nurses and treated them with respect. In the last few decades the standard uniforms were white uniform, hose, and shoes topped with a white cap representing the school from which they graduated. But as fashions changed over the years nurses are wearing uniform pantsuits or scrubs. The white uniform became a symbol of oppression and nurses abandoned their caps as impractical. Today, almost universally, nurses wear scrubs, which are relatively inexpensive, easily laundered, fit various body types, allow freedom of movement, and allow for individual expression.

The amount of training you'll need to become a nurse will vary depending on what area you want to specialize in, and much responsibility you want to have in your position. LPNs and LVNs generally need a professional license from an accredited program which takes from ten to twelve months to earn. If you want to become a registered nurse, however, there are several options available to you. Many nurses start out with an Associate Degree (ADN). This is typically an adequate starting place to find entry-level opportunities in most healthcare facilities. Other RNs choose to go on to their Bachelor of Science in Nursing, or BSN degree. In both of these degree programs, you'll be expected to pass courses in such subjects as anatomy and physiology, microbiology, chemistry, nutrition and psychology.

CHAPTER 2

Why I Want To Be A Nurse

Nursing is one of the greatest professions for those who are called to care for the sick and disabled. Nursing is one of the greatest profession for those willing to endure the hardships that is often required. As a young girl I was always taking care of my siblings and desired to pursue a nursing career. Starting my career as an LPN from a vocational school began working on a medical surgical unit. After working as an LPN for twelve years decided to return back to RN school. Being a LPN prepared me for the challenges that laid ahead for me in RN school. I am not saying this is the path you should take but it was better for me at the time, being a single mother raising two sons alone.

Any hospital experience will help develop an understanding of the responsibilities of a nurse. While working on a medical surgical unit I was blessed with a nurse manager who was so understanding and supportive who made nursing school so much easier. She gave me the schedule I needed to study and there was no stress about last minute changes. I couldn't of made it without her. I call her one of my angels. As a LPN I was able to learn the skills performed in a hospital, prioritize and organize my time, collaborate with other professionals, and document and record patient information. I Graduated from RN school in 1992 with my Associate Degree, then went on to complete my BSN 2004 and in 2009 received my Master Degree in Nursing Education. It has been a roller coaster ride but ended with a fulfilling and satisfying career. There are so many lovely memories of people I worked with professionally and are friends with to this day. The experience of a nursing career definitely has enriched my life and inspired me to want to share and demonstrate my true passion for nursing through my books, workshop and public speaking.

All nurses have a deep desire to help people. I am not only someone's caretaker but a confidante and trusted advisor to many people that came across my path in my nursing profession. The nursing profession offers certain flexibility that can lead to a longer, more sustainable career. You will have a job from a broad selection of specialties which include everything from critical care nursing to forensic nurse to anesthetic or remain at the bedside as a staff nurse. Nursing is considered the most trusted, ethically sound profession. From the flexibility to the multiple job opportunities this profession has the potential for a lifetime of rewards and you truly can impact lives for the better. You will have continuous and daily opportunities to make a difference in the lives of others. This along should inspire and encourage you to become passionate about the profession of nursing. You will literally have people relying and depending on you for the deliverance of the best possible care that leads to a safe recovery.

Mary Mahoney was the the first nurse of color was not only an inspiration for so many African American women, but to the entire nursing profession. Her drive and passion helped shape the standards the profession has become and continues to develop. I among thousands of other all over the world are what we are today because of the contributions of women like Mary Mahoney. Look at it this way, no matter the world changes, it will always need nurses, not only as bedside nurses but also for leadership roles, education and advocates. If you are unable to start as a RN, you can begin your career as a CNA (certified nursing assistant) to working your way to RN or even administrator.

As a nurse there are opportunities to care for the newborn to the critically ill elderly patient. To teach patients about their therapy, their diagnosis, about their medication and to remain healthy once discharged home from the hospital. Nursing is helping others with their needs and seeing them to better health. You will be involved in working in a health care setting with a promising career developing knowledge, practical skills and gaining experience. In pursuing this profession, your purpose is to help patients achieve their wellbeing and achieving their maximum potentials. I believe that the essence of this profession is achieving the knowledge and competency in performing nursing skills and interventions.

Nursing involves a combination of many disciplines, including aspects of biology and psychology to promote the restoration and maintenance of health in patients. And at the end of the day, behind the vital signs and doctor's order, what will count the most is much you really cared. Yes it's this caring which made this profession unique in the first place? The genuine reward of this work comes from the distinct gleam of the patient's eyes every time we perform what we have sworn to do. Although it is a sad fact that some nurses are quite amnesic to why they became nurses in the first place, the future nurses of today still, should rise and take the challenge of being a real nurse.

No one will ever tell you nursing is a stagnant profession. As a new graduate you will feel like you are scrambling to keep everything together with all the new procedures, technologies, treatments and processes. No matter what your specialty or your location, being an excellent multitasker, having empathy, and being obsessed with all the details always help you become a successful nurse. You will advance your career satisfying your goals of being your patient's best nurse. The best nurse thinks outside the box, adapting to changing situations, patient problems, unusual medication combinations, assessing and evaluating the whole picture. She uses her critical thinking skills developed in school and on the job to successfully carry her responsibilities with any assignment. Every nurse has to be organized and perform her duties in a planned manner to be successful.

There are a many reasons to choose nursing as a career. The work settings are endless. For example you can be a staff nurse in a hospital, a school nurse, work at a research facility, handle insurance claims from home and the list goes on and on. Nurses are the only profession who get to wear scrubs to work and be as comfortable as if they were wearing a pair of pajamas. After a few years of experience nurses will rarely have trouble finding a job even with the opportunity to travel all over the U.S. as a traveler, that's if you love to travel. Very few places allow their employees the chance to travel and work making high wages.

Nurses can be entrepreneurs due to the unique variety of skills and knowledge she acquire during her nursing career.

Nursing is the only professional discipline you can enjoy making a profound difference in lives everyday while working in a variety of medical settings. Nurses with high morals and a caring attitude contribute to this success. Nurses also contribute to the stability of the healthcare institutions and the wellbeing of their patients. Nurses not only give their book knowledge but a piece of their heart to each of her patients. It gives great satisfaction to invest in an industry that is expanding and enriching patient lives. Being a nurse you learn new things all through your career. It can be challenging to keep current on multiple medical trends. This training is to equip you to provide the best possible care for your patients. You get to learn from your colleagues and patients, which inspire you to explore deeper knowledge of the procedures and techniques you use. Nursing is such a broad field it will not be difficult for you to find the place that would allow you to utilize your interest in science as well to care for the sick. You will even experience different cultures to broaden your experience for all types of people.

For me there were no role models to follow in nursing. Inspired after taking a medical health course in high school realized the medical field would be the perfect career for me. The oldest of three children I was always taking care of my younger siblings had an innate desire to help people in times of need. Nursing definitely fit me as a career that offered diversity and learning. I will continue to face new challenges and believe in advancing education achieving new goals.

Chapter **3**

WHAT IS THE NURSING DISCIPLINE ?

If allegations against a nurse are proven, or he or she admits to the allegations, a board of nursing has the authority to discipline the nurse. The purpose of the discipline imposed is remediation; in other words, "to correct practice and promote safety". One of the least forms of discipline against a nurse is considered an "informal" or "non-public" discipline. Examples include an administrative warning letter. A reprimand or censure, the basis of which is improper conduct by the nurse, is a public discipline. The revocation of a nurse's license is the most serious discipline that can be imposed by a board of nursing. The nurse immediately loses his or her license and cannot legally practice nursing. Based on the board's requirements, the individual can apply for re-licensure. Requirements include a period of time before which re-licensure is not possible (e.g., 2 years) and the retaking of the NCLEX exam, as examples. It is important to note that re-licensure is at the board's discretion. Boards of nursing are required by federal law to report any adverse actions taken against a nurse licensee.

Florence Nightingale spoke first in 1859 on the nature of nursing and the need for knowledge distinct from medicine. She formed the earliest formation of nursing as a discipline. Nursing has been around for many years but the profession is still quite young. Florence Nightingale developed the idea that women needed to be trained as nurses. The first U.S. schools based on her model was opened in 1870s. Nursing education moved from the hospital to universities in the mid 1920's, and the number of baccalaureate programs in nursing remain small until the 1960's.

Since that time there has been substantial efforts to the development of a theory base for nursing. Increased interest in the nursing discipline body of knowledge has been evident in the last decade as seen by research from a nursing perspective. These efforts has served to advance the nursing discipline and also to challenge all nurses to articulate for themselves the theoretical foundations of their own practice. Nurses have long attempted to secure a unique identity for the profession. Many scholars are promoting an interdisciplinary framework for nursing practice.

The use of conceptual and theoretical frameworks to organize the educational curriculum of nursing programs is essential to protect and preserve the focus and clarity of nursing's distinct contribution to healthcare.

Nursing discipline means self control by which a nurse brings her behavior into agreement with the facility official behavior code or a facility can enforce nurse compliance with facility rules and regulations. The word discipline is derived from the Latin word meaning learning, teaching, and growing. It's defined as a training and molding of mind and character to work in accordance with certain recognized rules and regulations and customs. The objective of the nursing discipline is to obtain a willing acceptance of the rules and regulations and procedures of an organization. To impart an element of certainty despite several differences in informal behavior patterns. To develop among nurses a spirit of tolerance and a desire to make adjustments. To give and seek directions and responsibility. And to increase the working efficiency and morale of the nurses.

The principles of the nursing discipline is to ensure a disciplinary guide line to be in harmony with the ultimate goals of safe nursing care. It must be implemented through love and understanding not through fear. It should be primarily positive and constructive. It should ensure equal justice for all, respect the rights and dignity of an individual and humanitarian approach towards all. Disciplinary policies and procedures should be first preventive, then corrective but never retributive. The approach of discipline should be to place increasing responsibility on the nurse in terms of her own choices, purposes and behavior.

The nursing discipline has set a clearly developed purpose to serve the public and commitment to the individual and overall wellbeing of our society that directs the study and practice of nurses, educators and nurse scholars. Nursing is a caring discipline, although the role has changed over the years. Historically the nurse was seen as a nourishing and protecting person, who was willing to care for the ill, injured and elderly. She was also considered the female who took care of the children, which associated nursing with women. Through the years the role of the nurse moved from motherhood, nourishing children, towards a role of a person with rising responsibilities and expending tasks. Today nursing is related to caring for individuals in a healthcare related facility.

The nursing discipline according to its definition, all nurses and nurse leaders who conceptually coherent practices are joined to shape the next generation to consolidate and grow the body connected to nursing. We struggle continually explaining what it is we do to ourselves and those outside our profession. There are constant arguments regarding the Nursing theory and what constitutes Nursing knowledge. Lack of agreement has caused some confusion among nurses and caused many to dismiss the Nursing theory as irrelevant to everyday practice. Overall the

Nursing theory should provide the principles of a practice and a set of established statements or rules that are able to be tested.

A serious shortage of nursing has evolved due to multiple factors, mostly fewer young people are choosing a nursing career. Nursing has traditionally been a female dominated profession, but now have a greater range of career choices such as medical, law, business and engineering has increased tremendously. People often misunderstand the nursing discipline and if asked they think nurses just follow doctor's orders. But nurses assess the patient's condition, make critical decisions, provide life saving interventions, teach patients and families about caring for themselves, provide comfort and support and provide companionship. The nursing discipline is rated the most highly among professional whom the public trust. Ethics is an essential component of the nursing discipline. It ensures the safety of patients and their health and wellness of nurses and other healthcare providers.

Overall nurses remain the most trusted profession and should never take this trust for granted continuing to maintain this status. Trust involves integrity and honesty, the ability to rely on someone. Trust will always play an important role in the relationship between nurses and the patients she serves.

Chapter 4

HOW DO I PREPARE MYSELF?

First you have to be willing to sacrifice your time and family to studying long hours day and night. Preparation for nursing school should be way before you enter the classroom. Taking certain classes in high school will give you a head start on your prerequisites in college: English, Algebra and Geometry, Science including Biology and Chemistry, Physics and Computer Science are recommended, Social Studies, and two years of Foreign Language. Make sure you complete all of your prerequisites which will differ based on the program. Then double check with a program advisor or admissions counselor to ensure you're on track to meet the requirements for the program you chose to enter.

Be sure all of your immunization shots are up to date. Most colleges and universities require all incoming students to receive or sproof of the following:

1. Meningitis vaccination
2. Measles, mumps, rubella (MMR)
3. Varicella - chickenpox
4. Hepatitis B
5. Tetanus/Diphtheria/Pertussis
6. Seasonal flu
7. TB skin test

Many college courses consist of exams, papers, lab and deadlines. Managing your time is very important. You need to be organized and purposeful with your time to be successful in nursing school. To become a successful nurse you will need to learn to juggle these:

1. Exams
2. Quizzes

3. Clinicals

4. Care plans

5. Simulation labs

6. Skills check off

7. Certification

8. Reading assignments

9. Learn to take nursing school exams, choosing all that apply to question but choosing the best answer.

10. Pharmacology

11. Learning about nursing research and understanding evidence based practice.

12. Learn to write in APA format.

13. Learning medical terminology all while trying to understand the flow and culture of various health care facilities.

Networking with nurses you know and if you don't know any contact your local hospital about setting up an interview with nurses for information. Let them know you are a future nurse seeking information from nurses already in the field. Most would be glad to speak with you in an interview, email or over the phone. Prepare and have questions written out and keep the interview brief and professional. Be grateful at the end thanking the nurses for their time. You can also volunteer in the healthcare field in a hospital, nursing home, doctors office or clinic setting to determine if nursing appeal to you. Pay attention on the news relating to medical related and healthcare news sites and browse through them regularly. If you are serious about a nursing career you need to be aware of what's happening in that field.

You can join a nursing forum for participation and discussions and ask questions of the other nurses. It would be wise to get your financial budget in order, because nursing school can be expensive. For other support build a network of friends for help in advance such as a study buddy. If you are working let your supervisor know your requests to work your schedule around your school schedule. I am so thankful for having the sweetest nurse manager in the world. There was never any conflict with me having the days off I needed for school to study and prepare. She was truly and angel sent from God.

There is no doubt nursing school is challenging from the beginning to the end keeping you busy. It is important to prepare yourself as well as your family they wouldn't see you for a while. Being a single mom it was extremely hard with two young sons ages six and twelve to manage my life and raise them too. My older son was in the rebellious stage of transitioning into a teenager. It might be hard to understand but my younger son was more supportive and encouraging. He even brought the famous original poem, "Don't Quit" from school. Although I never knew where he got it. I was overwhelmed he cared enough about his mother and what I was going through. I stuck it on my refrigerator and looked at it every time walking through the kitchen.

Apologize to your spouses early if you are married, because there will be days you are going to be frustrated and may take it out on them. Fifty percent of the women in my class were going through separation and divorce. This is a extremely stressful ordeal for a couple to handle and most marriages or relationships end. Men can't handle the fact that you are now going to be independent and secure sometimes making more income than him. They are afraid you will not need him anymore. So they feel intimidated and insecure and don't know to approach the situation in a mature manner.

While you are preparing for your prerequisites, remember to prepare yourself emotionally and mentally for this long but worthwhile commitment. To prevent from becoming to stressful take time to still be you. You are more than a nursing student, but someone with various interests that you enjoy doing alone or with other people. Don't just drop everything when you start nursing school. Realize entering nursing school you are not going to learn everything while you are there. Your knowledge will come in steps once you graduate as you begin working on a unit. Always take school seriously and learn all that you can.

In nursing school a lot of times we neglect our bodies and mind. First thing in the morning spend a set amount of time for some quality time to meditate and feed your spirit. Say a prayer and read God's word. Instead of eating a lot of snacks and fast foods that's easy to get on the run start to develop healthy habits to keep your mind and body strong. Try developing a routine that includes a light breakfast, mediation and fitness. Get a friend and start a journal where you can express yourself on paper to decompress and share your frustrations openly and unfiltered without judgment is important.

Chapter **5**

HOW TO STUDY FOR EXAMS & PASS?

If you are wondering how do you suppose to retain so much information in such a short period of time maybe this chapter will help you understand? How will you juggle all the things you have to do along with studying versus getting enough sleep and not being too overwhelmed. I was a student nurse determined not to fail. If the instructor lectured on three chapters, I read each chapter two or three times. I didn't believe in shortcuts, cramming or memorizing the pages of my book. My whole philosophy was comprehension is the key. It was comprehension versus memorization. The only way to survive nursing school is to read the chapters to understand and comprehend what you read. This is to develop critical thinking skills, the foundation to dissecting nursing questions and passing exams. Retaining information through comprehension and understanding is what it takes to pass tests.

After being a nurse for 28 years realized there are a number of ways to prepare for exams. Start by reaching out to classmates to form a study group. This can become fun and the accountability of studying with others is a good way to make sure you are absorbing the material at a consistent rate. Your school is on your side and provide a variety of resources to help you achieve academic success. One well known resource is free tutoring centers where you can receive extra help on assignments and learn study techniques. Get familiar with your school library so you can know where to find the resources you might need throughout your nursing program. Schedule a certain time daily then you will more than likely commit yourself than if you tell yourself sooner or later. You can make it easier by programming a recurring daily study session in your phone and turn on the notification reminder.

When studying remember to understand this will be applied to clinicals and real life experiences. This will help you understand the material more. To ensure you understand reread the material. I would read every chapter three times making sure I comprehended everything. If there was something I didn't understand I made notes and asked questions during class during discussion time. Comprehension will take you further than memorization when it comes to critical thinking skills in real life experiences. There are hundreds of study tools to utilize to prepare you for passing exams. Apps like Quizlet offer flash cards, practice test and study guides. When you find yourself struggling with a particular nursing process, try using study tools to help you get through that hump.

When in class or clinical be engaged in every experience. Don't stand back and hold the wall or sat way back in the back of the classroom. In clinical the nurses on the unit will appreciate it and you will learn so much more if you take the initiative to do things. Volunteering for undesirable tasks will provide you with practical experience that is more valuable than any lesson in a book. It can be scary learning a new skill, but what better opportunity to learn while your instructors are there for support will give you the confidence you need to pass. If you make a mistake, just remember mistakes are part of the learning process.

The night before an exam be sure to get a good night rest and eat a healthy breakfast in the morning before leaving the house. Say a prayer just before the instructor hand out the exams. When taking the exam be sure to read each question slow and carefully. Do not rush through the questions. In the multiple choice questions there will always be more than one correct answer, but you have to pick the best answer by eliminating all the wrong answers. There are three components to understanding and to pass exams. You must understand the question. So if you haven't read your textbook this will be almost impossible. Ask yourself what is the question asking? Try not to jump to conclusions to quickly in the middle of reading a question. Rushing will definitely cause you to choose the wrong answer. Read the entire question, then read it again slowly and carefully. Look at your keywords like, "appropriate, highest priority, safe, therapeutic, accurate, next, first, best and indicated."

Choosing the most accurate answer in an exam can be tricky and if you get it wrong it could be you do not understand what the question's priority or best answer is. If this seem to be a major concern the best way to fix this is to practice as many questions as possible in NCLEX books. In preparation for my state board exam I answered at least 100 questions every day for ninety days and was successful passing the exam for the first time. Failing an exam could possibly be not because you didn't study enough but you just didn't prepare yourself.

On this important day it will be you versus the exam. You will be on your own; no books, no notes, no study friends and unable to ask the instructor to explain a process. This is time to concentrate and focus on the correct answer. If a question seem to be drawn toward the right answer, do not start rationalizing why this is not the correct answer. Most of the time it is the correct answer. Chances are you have already experienced a concept similar to this in all the reading and studying you've done in the past.

Let's face it in nursing school you can't get away from exam taking. You can not get through nursing school without having to sit and take some kind of test or exam. Many exams are multiple choice questions on paper or using a computer. Others may take be in the form of an oral test or a practical exercise to demonstrate skills learned. This is the only way to evaluate if you are competent and qualified to take care of the sick. No one can really tell you to get your own technique that's effective to help you pass tests. That's something you have to develop yourself by reading and researching about techniques and suggestions from people who have mastered the process.

Because results of exams and tests are so important, it's natural for a person to feel stressed on the big day. The key to performing your best at this crucial time is to do everything you can to minimize this stress. Throughout your studying and exam periods eat healthy and exercise regularly it will help to reduce your stress levels. It's tempting to grab quick and available junk food because you're too busy to prepare real meals. But a good night's sleep and a balanced diet can help improve your mental alertness and ability to study. Alcohol should be avoided the night before an exam as its effect is to dehydrate you. Drinking water during revision period and examinations is thought to improve academic performance.

The day before the exam always look at the bigger picture, as I have mentioned before, not isolated facts. Immerse in the subject rather than remembering individual facts. Rewrite your notes taken during lecture. Rewriting helps you take in key concepts, so restrict to writing the main points. When reading your textbooks write out brief points. In your study group discuss these key topics with your friends. Don't try to memorize, instead analyze the material so it is comprehended. If available to you read past exam papers to see the questions are worded and try to grasp what is being asked. Look for recurring themes from past papers so you have an idea of the kind of topics that come up again on future exams.

On the day of the exam arrive there with time to spare. This will give you time to get the seat you want and get comfortable and focused. When you receive your test, read the question slow and properly and try to retain your focus on the bigger picture. Do not panic and close your mind off to the many possibilities. Spend equally approximately five minutes on each question. Calmly read through each question and make a mark on those that you think are difficult so you can back to later. Allow yourself no more than five minutes for this. Give yourself a few minutes before the exam ends to make sure you're happy with what you've picked. Even if you don't change an answer you will feel better just rechecking. When it's all over turn the button off in your head. There is no need to stress further. You are through so breathe and relax. No matter you did, it's time to move on and prepare for the next one.

Chapter **6**

HOW DO I APPROACH MY INSTRUCTOR?

Nurse instructors are registered nurses with advanced education who have worked for many years before deciding to turn to a career of education. Most instructors have extensive clinical experience and may continue working after becoming educators. They usually serve as faculty in nursing schools and teaching hospitals, sharing their knowledge and skills to prepare the next generation of future nurses. They develop lesson plans, teach courses, evaluate educational programs, oversee students clinical practice and serve as role models.

Communicating with instructors sometimes could seem unbearable. If you have friends who have completed Nursing school that can share her experiences about past instructors would be wonderful. Share with her about you have built up this fear for instructors. When I taught as an clinical instructor my role was to prepare the student in becoming a competent nurse in the practice setting. PowerPoint presentations and lectures for clarification of information, additional wisdom and what important facts to focus on. Always engaging with my students whether through lecture or clinical performances lets them know I care. When they know you care about their welfare they're not intimidated.

When you find it unbearably intimidating to approach your instructor, maybe you should confront your fear. Not until you confront your fear will you be able to overcome it. One day after class voice your concerns with the instructor one on one basis and tell her you really feel. Remember your instructor is not there to mother you or make you feel good about yourself. She is there for one reason, to make sure you are a decently trained, fairly competent nurse when you graduate. You are over eighteen and fully grown and it's up to you to become all you can be as a successful skilled nurse. Once you get out in the real world it will still be up to you to advance in your career.

Your instructor was once in your same shoes with the same insecurities, so hopefully she will be considerate and supportive.

She know where you stand even though she may play the touch love rule. Most parents believe in this while raising their kids and can be effective if they stand their grounds. After raising two sons alone this rule does work the majority of the time. This rule when utilized by the instructor seem she is trying to break you down, but sometimes this is the only key to helping someone stand up and fight. By all means do not allow this to cause you failure as to quit. Just know you are not alone.

In the Nursing environment just as you don't get along with everyone, you probably will not get along with all the instructors. You will have those you love and make us love Nursing in a new light and then there are those no matter what you say or do it seem you two do not understand each other. Even though she play an integral part in your career, you have to consider what is your best interest. Do everything possible to prove you are competent and better yet prove it to yourself.

In LPN school there were instructors who were intimidating for me and others in my class. Later I learned this has gone on for many years. It's not something students just make up. One particular day in clinical, Labor & Delivery I was instructed to insert a Foley catheter in a patient who was in labor. Never having performed this procedure there was no support from my instructor. Instead she stood back with her arms folded. When I contaminated the sterile field she stated, "Stop you have contaminated your sterile field." And if that wasn't enough the following day I was placed on probation. With a lot of prayers and trusting in God, He brought me through and I passed the course.

Nursing instructors should strive to be effective instructors whether in the hospital or classroom setting demonstrating astute interpersonal skills, clinical competency, professionalism and principles of adult learning. She should have personality traits that are attentive, nurturing, demonstrating concern about her students, encouraging demeanor, mentoring approach and supportive. Excellent nurse educators should have strong leadership and communication skills and outstanding theoretical and clinical knowledge. Most are intelligent, creative, competent and fair. They are usually lifelong learners and have such a huge passion to pass it onto her students.

A student should never be afraid to approach her instructors. They are your resource and you must overcome your fears and start talking directly to them in and outside of the classroom. Once you get comfortable confronting her you'll discover she is human too. Always be prepared with what you have to ask her, remember they are very busy and not mind readers. Have your questions prepared in advance and able to articulate clearly what you want. Be honest with her. The more truthful and open you are the more receptive your instructors will be to assist you in your academic need. Call them by their right title and name when addressing them. Most will inform you on the first day what they want to be called. By all means avoid approaching them aggressively and please don't whine. Don't act entitled, she is not your employee or your mother. Watch you phrase your words, so as not to sound like you're asking for special treatment or inside answers. Don't ask the impossible of your instructors, because they are restricted by course and departmental policies.

One of the key strategies of students' successful learning is the influence and role model of the instructors. Good communication between the two will help to make the teaching and learning process easier. It is an integral part of nursing and is the foundation for the provision of high quality nursing care. So the instructor's job is to convey this effectively to her students to develop excellent and interpersonal skills. Communication must always be safe, effective compassionate and respectful. This is understood and evaluated in clinical practice continuous both through self reflection and personal development.

Chapter 7

THE FEAR OF FAILURE

There are so many potential nursing students who have a desire to pursue the nursing career but never take the initiative to apply. One of their biggest fear is the fear of failure. They either have had a friend to fail in nursing school or heard horror stories difficult it was to pass. We've all heard about those horror stories and challenges you would face, but in reality, most of these stories are inaccurate or greatly exaggerated.

Don't get it wrong, from my experience nursing school was one of the most challenging and difficult thing I have ever done in my life. It took many long hours of commitment to reading and studying. There was constant fear of failing but refused to let that stand in my way. The desire to become a nurse was much stronger than to turn away from my dream. Yes there are people who fail. Most of the time they fail because they didn't want to put the time in to study. Some even dropped out completely, later realizing nursing isn't for them or it was too boring. Reflecting back on my fears they were never justified and passed with honors.

Then too there are those who graduate with flying colors and feel it was the best choice they ever made. Nursing is one of the fastest growing profession and millions say, it isn't that hard. It's all much you apply yourself in your books. If you enjoy the healthcare field, and you are willing to put forth the effort and time you can succeed and make it. But if you refuse to study, don't attend class then Nursing is not for you and it will be incredibly hard. If you think you could never pass the difficult courses and have no medical experience it would be an excellent idea to start in positions like nursing assistant or phlebotomist before tackling a Nursing career. I began my nursing career as a nursing assistant and later became an LPN. This path prepared me tremendously for the healthcare field. Working in these positions I received excellent clinical experience before enrolling into a RN program. I was familiar with the duties of a nurse in the hospital, doctors office or nursing home. This path puts you ahead of the other students who has no healthcare background.

The fear of failure is a normal emotion and for every pursuit you will experience fear in life. It doesn't make a difference if it is Nursing, law, teaching, accountant or parenting, we are all human and experience fear of failure because it make us feel worthless. You must learn to channel that fear into a productive attitude. If you constantly dwell on the fear and allow it to consume you the negative thoughts will cause you to give up. Keep your fear in the proper perspective and channel that energy to help you study more. The more test you pass and the closer you get to completing the program your fear will start to subside and your confidence will begin to build and fear will continue to leave.

The most that can happen if you fail is you can always retake the class or get a tutor. Many wonderful and successful nurses have retaken a class. The key is as long as you attend class, lectures and put in ample time to study and do your homework you have excellent odds to passing the program. If you have the desire to be a nurse you have won half the battle. If there is a heartfelt desire after spending time in the hospital when you were young due to an illness, you discovered your passion you will do great as a nursing student. There are many wonderful rewards to help you get over your fears. You have the benefits of flexible scheduling, many career paths and specialties, not to mention the job security. Let's face it, there are always some risks and failure in any career but nursing is a life long passion and not just a job. No matter what your reasons are to pursue a career, just know that being a nurse offers practical benefits, emotional rewards, but what matters most is the care you will provide at the bedside for the patient every day.

Nursing school is a big decision and there are many reasons to pursue a career in Nursing. First decide if you are willing to put in the time and effort required to complete the program? Second are you willing to put your family and life on hold? In LPN school I remember coming home and fixed my sons dinner and going straight to my books to study. Sitting at the table with my books spread out I would study for hours and hours at a time. You have to face the fears because they are not going away in nursing school. Looking back with all the fears and questions I'm still glad I made the decision to choose nursing as my career.

If you have a fear or phobia of blood starting IVs or giving injections this should not keep you from becoming a nurse. This fear is because you have never done it before. The more exposure would definitely help unless there are severe phobias. If you genuinely love taking care of the sick and helping others, it's obvious a nursing career is right for you. I strongly encourage and support you to pursue this field. If you find yourself considering not to go after your dream career because of this fear of blood and needles, please rethink this. This happens to hundreds of nurses but overtime you will surely break yourself of this fear. My point is you can desensitize yourself of this fear. You do need to ask yourself if you can stand seeing it daily.

Blood is one of the many bodily fluids nurses deal with on a daily basis. Students come in close contact with blood, urine, stool, sputum during clinical rotations. This will be only a glimpse of the unglamorous part of the job, but the many rewards will outweigh this. Starting IVs can be scary but just as any other skill the more you perform the more comfortable you become with most skills. When we are performing this skill we long to see a flash of blood in the chamber. Learning to start IVs is one of the most exciting skills you can perform and the better you are your reputation gets high ratings on your unit.

Why are IVs so intimidating to some nurses? To get rid of this fear try spending hours in the skills lab practicing on the big plastic arm with the huge vein with a thousand needle sticks all along it. You can also try watching video on YouTube videos. But there is nothing compared to starting one on a real human patient. Way after you become a nurse sometimes it will happen and sometimes it will not no matter long you have been a nurse.

When it comes to starting IVs there are three C's: Comfortable, Consistency and Confidence. First become comfortable with the equipment used to start an IV. Play with it safely. Take apart the needle and catheter. Practice putting on a tourniquet. Get use to the feel of holding and advancing an IV catheter. Learn it feels to hold one. Also it is important to get use to what veins look and feel like. Feel your nursing friends veins. Learn where veins are anatomically.

Once you start feeling veins, it becomes an addiction. Once you are done playing around with IV needles and equipment, pick a method that works for you. Get use to setting up your supplies the same way. Familiarity improves quality work and perfection. Then last is building your confidence while getting over the fear of missing the vein is the main struggle. Once you tell yourself you can do it and it's okay to miss your confidence will elevate to new levels. Don't let the fear deter you from even trying. The only way to improve is practice.

Entering nursing school should be an exciting and challenging journey in your life. Being a novice and overcoming your fear of failure on to become a successful adult student is great. Getting through the fear of nursing school is a skill you can learn. I understand this may not be easy for everyone. You have to be ready to face your fears to transcend them. Become aware of your specific fears that seem to causing havoc in your life. It is so easy to be attached to your fearful thoughts and feelings, but you must know you are not your fears.

The most basic meaning of fear is an emotion induced by a perceived threat. Fear causes a change in the brain functions and change in behavior. We are often fearful of a possible outcome, even though there might not be any real danger. Tiptoeing around our fears might work but I'm claiming this to be very ineffective. Sadly most people do not deal with their fears, often crippling them preventing them from achieving their full potential, even disabling them from doing what they need to do.

You can either focus on analyzing and understanding your fears or you can suppress it and avoid facing it. The only true solution to overcoming fear is to embrace it. There is no getting rid of fear, it is a natural part of life, which alerts you to possible dangers and brings out your survival instincts.

Chapter 8

WHAT DOES A GOOD NURSE LOOK LIKE?

A good nurse have a deep seated desire and compassion to serve and help those who can't help themselves. Nursing is a calling from God and considered to be a ministry to serve. A good nurse is someone who holds a patient's hand just before they are wheeled off for a surgical procedure, while listening to their concerns with empathy. Or comforting a child frightened in the hospital emergency room. A good nurse has a deep awareness of someone else's suffering without judgment, which is a root of compassion. Research has shown that a nurse's compassion can lessen a patient's suffering who is on the frontline to do something daily to make a difference in a person's life. These are just a few examples of a good nurse.

The nursing profession is about kindness and caring for the whole person as it is about medical and technical knowledge. The traits of a good nurse some will come naturally while others may be strengthened through education. Together these traits makes a successful professional nurse. A good nurse recognize situations when patients are understandably anxious or upset, and helping them maintain their dignity. This requires honest communication saying what you mean in a caring and gentle tone, behaving fairly and ethically in every situation. A good nurse is able to make quick decisions in a medical crisis keeping her cool and remaining level headed. Your education play a vital role here. When you are knowledgeable about the technical aspect of your job you'll be better equipped to make hard decisions while remaining calm. You will make rational decisions during stress and adversity.

Good nurses are detailed and meticulous when it comes to giving information, instructions and giving medications. Doctors and patients rely on good nurses to be focus and careful. Proper communication is more important than giving medication or starting an IV. Good nurses are expected to talk to patients and help them understand medical situations which can be complex and scary to the person going through such tribulations. Good nurses are clear communicators who truly listen to their patients making sure to acknowledge all of their needs.

A good nurse is dedicated and caring in a field that is demanding both emotionally and physically. She recognizes the benefits and rewards does outweigh the challenges. To become a good nurse there's a lot of technical and clinical information you'll need as a nurse: critical thinking and communication skills, patient assessment skills, understanding disease management protocols and development of care plans. No other profession offers so much while making a profound difference in the lives of people who needs and appreciate it. Good nurses gives a piece of their hearts to every patient and contribute success and stability of healthcare facilities. Good nurses are team-oriented, lifelong learners, assertive and have a positive attitude.

A good nurse has the ability to be team-oriented and able to collaborate with other nurses when it comes to delegation, crisis and her schedule. Working long hours and with so many nurses needs, often nurses are asked to work overtime or switch their schedule to sufficiently staff her unit. Nurses are employed to care for the sick and wounded and when they band together their work is twice as effective for the good of their patients. Whether you are part of a care team made up of multiple healthcare experts like a physical therapist or nutritionist, it's important to know teamwork is essential to getting the job done right improving the patient's health.

Nurses have to be adaptable and flexible to jump in to assist another nurse who is struggling with her patient workload. Healthcare is a complex industry requiring the coordination of multiple individuals to help provide better support for co-workers, for patients during times of stress. The typical health team is made up of registered nurses, licensed practical nurses, nursing assistants and unit secretaries. When all is working together, this model of nursing will help prevent errors and help nurses reach optimal healthcare. Good teamwork must consist of good communication between nurses when changing shifts by passing on clear and detailed information.

Good nurses are safe maintaining patient safety by protecting them in a hazardous environment such as infection, blood borne diseases and psychological distress. First there has to be the presence of healthy and well rested nurses which is critical to providing vigilant monitoring, emphatic patient care. A good nurse will practice professionalism that reduces the probability of an adverse event. Patient safety is the cornerstone of high quality care. Nurses are critical for their surveillance and coordination that reduce negative outcomes as mortality and morbidity. High quality care is the umbrella under which patient safety resides. The Institute of Medicine (IOM) of patient safety is defined as the prevention of harms to patients. Emphasis of delivery of care that: 1) prevents errors 2) learn from the errors that do occur 3) is built on a culture of safety that involves healthcare professionals, organizations and patients. Patient safety is essential and a vital component for not only nurses but ultimately all disciplines. All disciplines are responsible to see that no harm occurs to patients. The nursing shortage has a major impact on patient safety endangering quality of care. This places patients at risk and undermines the entire healthcare industry.

Good nurses are lifelong learners and believe in a positive perspective on learning and is an important quality of a good nurse. She takes every opportunity for continued education or pursuing advanced education. Educational background in my family history has opened many doors for this generation that my blue collar family were not allowed and far beyond reaching. Advanced education and increased education is essential to match the transformation occurring in the United States healthcare in the practices clinicians follow to achieve improved outcomes. Education is needed before and after receiving licenses, because nursing is an occupation that is changing rapidly in technology and research. In hospitals continuing education is a form of lifelong learning for all employees. It helps keep up to date with the latest knowledge and advances in healthcare. It is proven that continuing education in the health professions is effective in improving healthcare, patient outcomes and population health.

Lifelong learning is a dynamic process which encompasses both personal and professional life. It allows a good nurse to appreciate new ideas in order to gain a new perspective. The most essential elements of a lifelong learner are reflection, questioning, understanding the dynamic nature of knowledge and engaging in learning by seeking learning opportunities. Its very rare to see a nurse who chooses not to apply his or her mind towards the goals of constant learning and professional growth. A nurse's lifelong learning journey begins in nursing school, setting the appetite of what's to come. Good nurses see nursing as a way of life, soaking up information at a conference or taking an online course, reading magazines. Nurses never stop learning, ever.

As a nurse you will never stop being a student of the work, especially when it comes to communication, adapt and lead. In communication, a fundamental skill, is an art, requires continual practice. Everyday will present tons of different situations and patients, all require effective communication. A good nurse learn to adapt to the constant change in technology, patient care models and new treatments and she knows if she doesn't she will be left behind. Good nurses who take interests away from the bedside further their education, ask questions or pursue leadership positions are influential, credible and irreplaceable.

Assertiveness with kindness and compassion are certainly qualities of a good nurse is important. She needs to be a bit bossy and give clear, firm directions to those they work with. Remember there is a slight difference in assertive and aggressive. Assertive is a useful skill in life and can be beneficial on a nursing unit in a leadership position. Be confident, not pushy. When approaching people have confidence in yourself, whether with another nurse, a difficult doctor or a hurting patient. You can't pull away from confrontation and fall into a passive communication style because in nursing you are talking to people all the times. A good nurse is able to get her opinion across and let the other person know what you want done. She makes sure a fair outcome is achieved where all opinions are taken into consideration by listening to the patient or the doctor to make the right decision.

Along with being assertive and confident a good nurse values herself and her profession. It's about believing you are entitled to basic rights as a human being and a healthcare professional. Being assertive can lead to increased respect and recognition as a person and as a nurse. Being assertive is not about being combative or aggressive. It's about holding a belief that you're someone who matters. It will make you feel more confident and help you get the respect you and your profession deserve. Assertive is another mode of communication characterized by a confident affirmation of a statement without need of proof. Assertiveness is essential for nurses to build effective team relationships. It is described as expressing thoughts and feelings without denying the rights of others. Nurses are able to inform others of their needs effectively without causing offense to others. It has been found assertive nurses are most likely to provide appropriate care and improve the quality of care.

A positive attitude is another essential quality that makes a good nurse. Attitude is everything because a nurse is typically the healthcare professional that patients spend the most time with. She is often on the frontline of care and setting the tone and mood for healing with their optimism, compassion and critical thinking skills. If you talk to a good nurse she will probably point to a mentor or preceptor who helped them along the way. Someone who has overcome the challenges that go along with being a nurse can be invaluable in helping you succeed. A positive attitude and demeanor is spectacular affecting her patients by everything she does. In nursing a positive attitude is a not a choice but a necessity. In any job your attitude is important! In nursing a good attitude makes patients feel you have their best interest.

Your knowledge, experience and skills may have landed you the job but don't underestimate important your good attitude and interpersonal skills have on the outcome. If you find yourself consistently in a bad mood, step back and examine the situation. Ask yourself what is causing the distress? Could it be something at home transferring to work? Are you burnt out? Do you have a issue with a specific co-worker? Nurses are the backbone of every unit. In the hospital it is imperative patients receive the best care from the best people. A positive attitude can increase the consistency of high performance and patient satisfaction. Nurses with poor attitude tend to have a higher probability of mistakes.

The best way to advance your career and earn s good reputation is through a good attitude. Your attitude influence all areas of your day to day life and determines well you handle stress. You will encounter many challenges and stressors in the workplace; long hours, rotating shifts, inadequate staffing, poor teamwork and pressure to achieve higher performance in an emotionally and demanding career.

Chapter **9**

THE REWARDS OF A NURSING CAREER

There are so many rewards in nursing that its impossible to put them all in this chapter. Each reward that merits mentioning is experienced by each nurse in a very unique way. First having a career that is financially stable is very rewarding plus security. But to have a career in nursing can be personally rewarding also. Choosing nursing as your career can provide the best of two worlds. A flexibility in schedules, benefits, job security and personal fulfillment. You will be privileged to help and care for the injured, sick and dying. This gives you the opportunity to make a difference in the lives of others.

A career in nursing may seem overwhelming at first with all the classes, exams and skills labs, however once you start your nursing experience will become rewarding. Nursing is a unique profession that gives us the ability to enhance lives and encourage wellness. There will be strong relationships and emotional ties developed with coworkers who become like family creating lasting memories. Your patients and family members are a blessing that will be with you for many years. There will be difficult times when the deaths of loved ones who were married over fifty years can be overwhelming for the family and spouse and even yourself. It is the nurse's responsibility during the death process to make sure the patient isn't suffering. There are standing orders for various medications to provide comfort for the patient in their time of death. Then on the other end of the spectrum the nurse is usually the one to tell family about the death of their loved ones. Assisting them with he funeral arrangements can be a sad experience but at the same time fulfilling to help console them with their needs.

It is a blessing to be part of anyone's birth and equally a blessing to be a part of a death. You may have to be a confidante for a patient who has no one else to share their personal and private problems. Sometimes being a good listener gives the patient comfort and reassurance. As a nurse you will be involved with some very precious moments such as assisting bringing a new baby into the world and handing it to the mother for the first time. You have an opportunity to be attentive, compassionate and a good listener to someone who really depends on you being there when they have no one else.

After taking care of a patient and they return to your unit with flowers and cake to thank you for the kindness you bestowed upon them can be such a rewarding experience you may never forget. With such rewards you will learn you are the one who benefits feeling profoundly appreciated knowing you have made a difference in someone's life. "The miracle is not that we do this work, but that we are happy to do it." -Mother Teresa. One of the most favorite rewards is when you are out taking care of errands and you run into a former patient and they not only remember the excellent care you gave but they also remember your name and want to give you a hug.

Nursing can be rewarding because it will bring you into the lives of people who you would never have met if you were not a nurse. You will have tangible satisfaction helping others when they are sick and making a difference in the lives of others. When caring for a patient and they begin to recover you feel good inside for an opportunity to provide emotional support by holding their hand through a trying experience and tragedy. Nursing is the most rewarding, diverse and flexible career with numerous opportunities to expand in a wide variety of avenues to choose from. I have experienced every specialty from medical surgery, intensive care, emergency room, post operative care and education. Now working part-time in a hospital on the float pool enjoy the satisfaction of still promoting health care and making difference in lives today. I also write books to inspire, motivate and encourage the oncoming generation of nurses and women.

Nursing is an rewarding career that you will make a difference in someone's life while guiding them back to better health. All of your hard work is worthwhile when you see one of your patients who once needed total care regimen regain their independence. Nurses experience more than one reward each day.

One of your most important personal rewarding experiences are the knowledge and training you had to rake and strake through hours of studying that's able to help you save lives. You know also you have the knowledge to help your family, friend, or people you meet in your everyday life.

The special and professional training prepares you for making responses to emergencies automatic and your actions certain. Saving individual lives is rewarding in and of itself by performing your duties day after day is amazing and rewarding. Emotionally you become your patients confidante. Caring for patients regularly and monitoring their condition a trust relationship develops. You become a listening ear when the patient's loved one is not at the bedside. You can only hold their hand without saying a word, means a lot to someone going through physical and mental pain. Even when the patient does not express their gratitude, the nurse feels emotionally rewarded because she knows she is doing more than what her duty requires.

While nursing is a lucrative career that provides financial stability it might not be the right occupation for everyone. If you have read to this point in this book you are nursing material. You have a desire to help others in a nurturing manner which you will find satisfying on a personal and professional level.

CHAPTER **10**

How To Advance In My Nursing Career?

Once you become a registered nurse there will be multiple options to choose from as a leader in healthcare. Ask yourself after working as a nurse for a year, where do I want to be in five, ten or fifteen years from today? If you are open to advance learning this will give you the confidence to take on many different nursing roles over the years. Education is important in advancing your career. With each degree or certificate in a specialized nursing will open more doors for new opportunities, to help you find the perfect job for you.

Working as a LPN and simultaneously taking the stepladder approach to nursing education I pursued an Associate Degree in Nursing. Working as a RN attained a Bachelors Degree in Nursing, and later achieved a Masters Degree in Nursing Education. There is increased importance for advanced degrees, because most positions in advance practice, leadership, teaching and research requires Masters and Doctoral degrees. Learn to network within your workplace, meeting new people exchanging new ideas and gain information about new approaches to solve problems. Discuss new options with other nurses focusing and sharing the same interest.

Take opportunities to join professional networks which is crucial in our society. As our world is rapidly changing on a daily basis, global networking with others is becoming more to businesses connect with other disciplines. While networking is an important way to advance your career it is a clear way of learning new ideas. Establish a mentoring relationship over a gradual time period. You can be a mentee to someone who you feel comfortable with and whom you consider a role model. You can ask the mentor for career advice, suggestions and guidance to help you as a new nurse on her unit. There are many mentoring programs to join ran by organizations such as AONE. You can also join research groups, journal clubs and volunteering on special projects as a way to meet people who can mentor you.

Always pursue professionalism during your career which builds your reputation and character. The key components of nursing professionalism is honesty, maintaining patient confidentiality, offering respect for individuals, cultivating strong interpersonal skills in dealing with people, keeping a positive attitude, maintaining competency and keeping up to date in one's work. Ethics is another cornerstone of nursing professionalism. As a nurse ethics should be understood because it influences the decisions and health of our patients. Investing your nursing career today will be what you will put into practice tomorrow.

Maintaining a strong nursing workplace is essential to meeting the needs of diverse populations and advancing global health. The shortage places great danger that result when few nurses are available to provide care. Nursing education at all levels are needed to fill roles in the health care system. Nurses need to provide better understanding of and experience in care management, quality improvement methods, system level change management, and the roles of nurses in a reformed healthcare system.

Once you are a nurse focus first on getting better and making sure you have a comfortable handle on your responsibilities is important for success. Advancing in your career is a way to continue to get better, improve your professional prospects and challenge yourself, to have better options in the years to come. Working as a nurse find ways to stand out and separate yourself from your peers to become trusted and respected. Being professional, reliable and proficient by working hard will earn recognition from your supervisors and become a candidate should a new position arise. In most jobs if an individual respect the company's values, provide excellent customer service and are consistent are the ones sought after first.

One of the greatest things about the nursing discipline is the unlimited supply of choices and opportunities. Picking which path to take is not that simple. I would advise you to do further research and decide if this is the path you want to take. Here are a few options:

1. **Nurse Practitioner Entry Requirements**
   - You must be a registered nurse (RN).
   - You must hold a hospital diploma, an associate degree in nursing, or a bachelor's degree.
   - Two years of work experience are required for nurse practitioner specializations.

NURSE PRACTITIONER CAREER BASICS

Nurse practitioners (NPs) are a type of Advanced Practice Registered Nurse (APRN) whose specialized education and clinical training allow them to provide higher levels of care and perform a variety of tasks that RNs are not licensed to do. Nurse practitioners often focus on specific areas or populations, including pediatrics, geriatrics, mental health or adult medicine. They may complete an advanced degree program that allows them to practice independently and take on roles similar to that of a doctor.

Labor Statistics (BLS) reports that the mean annual wage for nurse practitioners was $97,990 in May 2014, with those who work in hospitals earning the most. APRNs enjoy additional benefits such as flexible work schedules, educational opportunities and even child care services.

1. **Nurse Educator**

Master of Science in Nursing – Nurse Educator, will

prepare you for a cutting-edge career that combines a passion for nursing and teaching. Through the program, you will be equipped with the critical thinking skills and knowledge needed to promote the profession of nursing through teaching, clinical practice, program development and implementation, and scholarship.

You also will develop skills relevant in:

- Evaluation strategies.
- Population health management.
- Health policy and ethics.

Potential Career Options:

- Clinical Nurse Specialist
- Nursing Administrator
- Undergraduate University Nursing Professor

You may also be interested in exploring a master degree in Public Health, Healthcare

1. **Clinical Nurse Specialist Clinical (CNSs)** provide direct care to patients in one of a range of specialties, such as pediatrics, geriatrics, emergency care and oncology. CNSs may also

serve as consultants, assisting other medical professionals working to improve patient outcomes and influence all levels of care. The National Association of Clinical Nurse Specialists (NACNS) describes CNS specialties in terms of population, setting, disease or medical subspecialty, type of care, and type of problem. **This career is categorized as an advance practice registered nurse (APRN) role because it requires graduate-level education and clinical training.**

CNSs spend 2-3 more years in school, beyond the requirements for RN licensure, completing master's or doctoral degrees. Due to the high level of precision and knowledge demanded of them, CNSs are often relied upon to advise other nurses and serve in leadership roles.

Daily Responsibilities

- Observes patient condition and diagnoses problems and illnesses
- Orders medical tests and evaluates results

- Treats diseases, injuries, and disabilities associated with the area of expertise
- Advises nurses and other medical staff members on patient care issues
- Promotes disease prevention and wellness
- Conducts research to further knowledge about the area of specialty
- Conducts physical exams

1. <u>Nurse Manager</u> organize and direct the activities of nursing units in hospitals, nursing homes and other healthcare facilities. They perform a variety of administrative activities and ensure that all nurses in their units provide high-quality care to patients. In 2010, the average salary of a full-time nurse manager was $82,090 a year, according to a survey conducted by the editors of the journal "Nursing Management." A nurse must meet several requirements to qualify for this position.

Education

The minimum educational requirement for nurse managers varies from one employer to another. Some employers will allow an experienced RN to assume the role of nurse manager without completing a baccalaureate degree. Other employers require a minimum of a bachelor's degree in nursing. The American Nurses Credentialing Center administers the Magnet program, which recognizes qualifying medical facilities for excellence in nursing. Starting January 1, 2013, 100 percent of a hospital's nurse managers must have baccalaureate or graduate degrees in nursing for the facility to qualify for this program. As more employers seek Magnet status, more nurses will need to earn baccalaureate degrees if they wish to become nurse managers.

Experience

All nurse managers must have experience delivering bedside care to patients. Most hospitals require at least two years of nursing experience before a nurse qualifies for this position. Some employers require as many as three to five years of experience.

Every nurse manager must also have a valid RN license in good standing.

1. <u>Nursing Informatics</u> **To enter the field of health informatics, nurses typically need at least a bachelor's degree in nursing and experience working with electronic healthcare records.** However, the job is so specialized and focused that many employers prefer job applicants who have earned a Master's degree in Health Informatics, Healthcare Management or Quality Management. Nurses who attain a degree in nursing administration with an emphasis on health informatics may also qualify for many jobs.

Courses in the USF programs include Integrated <u>Electronic Health Records</u>, Medicine Business Models, Managerial Communication, Basis Statistics and Clinical Systems Applications and <u>Project Management</u>.

Many employers prefer nurses for health informatics positions, because nurses have knowledge of the medical profession. It can be easier to train nurses on the technological aspects of the job rather than teaching someone with the technical skills all the details of the healthcare system.

Nurses who specialize in nursing informatics, a specialized field of the health informatics sector, will combine skills in health science, computer science and information technology to help healthcare providers store, retrieve and utilize large amounts of data as it applies to patient care.

Nursing informatics professionals also simplify documentation of patient care and enter patient notes using computers, mobile devices and voice recognition software. Nursing Informatics professionals aim to improve the accuracy of patient data and enable critical data analysis to improve efficiency of overall patient care.

Nursing is an honorable and still growing profession, but advancement in the field can sometimes be difficult. Here are a few critical guidelines to help you on your journey toward success as a nursing informatics professional.

1. **Master in Nursing Specialty** (acute care, adult, family, geriatrics, neonatal, palliative)

a) <u>Geriatrics</u> Students spend time in the classroom studying advanced theoretical nursing concepts and research. Some programs allow students to focus their studies on specialty areas. They apply this knowledge in clinical settings, such as hospitals, long-term care facilities and specialty clinics, where they work under the supervision of experienced professionals. Some common classes may include:

- Disease prevention and Illness Management
- Health assessment
- Advanced pathophysiology
- Pharmacology
- Human development
- Physiologic aging

Employment Outlook and Salary

The U.S. Bureau of Labor Statistics (BLS) doesn't collect data specifically on nurse practitioners, but it does collect data on RNs and include nurse practitioners in this category. Between 2014 and 2024, employment for RNs was expected to increase 16%, according to the BLS, because more people are living longer and are more likely to need health care. These aging populations are also seeking more outpatient care, which creates a higher demand for nurses in home health care, residential care facilities and nursing homes. The BLS also reported that advanced nurse practitioners should be in high demand, especially in areas lacking sufficient health care, such as urban and rural areas. Nurse practitioners can act as primary health care providers to those struggling to afford medical services.

According to BLS May 2015 data, all RNs made a median salary of $67,490. Those in the 75th percentile earned $82,490 annually, and those in the 90th percentile earned $101,630 each year. RNs working in specialty industries, other than psychiatric and substance abuse, earned an average salary of $76,310. As of August 2016, Salary.com reported that nurse practitioners earned a median salary of $99,865.

b) Acute Care: An acute care nurse practitioner (ACNP) provides advanced nursing care to patients suffering brief but severe illnesses, typically in an emergency department, ambulatory care clinic or other short term stay facility. ACNPs diagnose and treat acute medical conditions, working in collaboration with the physician and other members of the health care team. The ACNP profession is one of the more fast-paced nursing career choices, and it is loaded with responsibility and variety.

Degree you'll need to practice: Master of Science in Nursing (MSN)

Certification: Must be certified by your State Board of Nursing or receive a national certification from an agency such as the American Nurses Credentialing Center or the American Academy of Nurse Practitioners.

Median annual salary: $100,910*

ACNPs are nurse practitioners (NPs) with a specialty in acute care nursing.

Acute care nurse practitioners must first complete a 2- or 4-year degree in nursing and be licensed as registered nurses (RNs). Most gain experience as acute care RNs before returning to school to earn an advanced degree and become Advanced Practice Nurses (APNs).

To become an acute care nurse practitioner, you will also need to meet these requirements:

- You will need to get a Master of Science in Nursing (MSN) degree that includes specialized ACNP coursework. Nursing schools usually offer this degree as a 2-year program with about 40 credit hours of coursework, plus hundreds of clinical study hours.

- If you already have a master's degree in nursing, you may be able to prepare for ACNP certification with a 1-year post-master's program.

- Once you have completed your nursing school training, you must become certified by your State Board of Nursing or receive a national certification from an agency such as the American Nurses Credentialing Center or the American Academy of Nurse Practitioners.

b)<u>adult family</u>: You'll handle duties commonly performed by a physician, often partnering with patients throughout the family life cycle. You'll offer education and counseling as well as tests and procedures and be trained to provide a wide range of care to a diverse group of patients. You'll focus on health promotion and disease prevention beginning in childhood and continuing throughout the aging process, and diagnose and develop treatment plans for acute and chronic diseases.

Where you'll work: Clinics, private offices, hospice centers, nurse-managed health centers, schools, homes

Degree you'll need to practice: Master's degree and certification by your State Board of Nursing

Median annual salary: $107,460*

FNPs are nurse practitioners (NPs) with a specialty in family medicine.

Most family nurse practitioners spend their early years as RNs or BSNs then go back to school to earn their master's degree and become an Advanced Practice Nurse (APN). APNs are specialized nurses with masters or doctorate level training that deliver services that are commonly delivered by physicians. In addition to FNP, here are three other titles that APNs can earn:

- <u>Certified Nurse Anesthetist</u> — Administer anesthesia to surgery patients

- <u>Certified Nurse Midwife</u> — Provide prenatal care and deliver babies

- <u>Clinical Nurse Specialist</u> — Provide basic or specialized care

If you would like to become a family nurse practitioner, you will need a Master of Science in Nursing degree. Then you must become certified by your State Board of Nursing or receive a national certification offered by a variety of agencies, including the American Nurses Credentialing Center and the American Academy of Nurse Practitioners.

Master's Nursing Program Curriculums

The Commission on Collegiate Nursing Education (CCNE) and the National League for Nursing Accrediting Commission (NLNAC) have accredited more than 330 master's degree programs. There are a variety of available programs, including the Master of Science in Nursing (MSN) degree, Master of Nursing (MN) degree, Master of Science (MS) degree with a major in nursing, or Master of Arts

(MA) degree with a nursing major. The requirements for each degree depends on the institution providing the program. If you already have a hospital diploma or associate's degree, there are accelerated programs that allow RNs to earn their baccalaureate and master's degree in one program. Some universities also offer joint-degree programs, such as a master's in nursing combined with a Master of Business Administration, Master of Public Health, or Master of Hospital Administration.

c)neonatal Care

What you'll do: Neonatal nurse specialists focus on the care of newborn infants. They may care for healthy infants, provide focused care for premature or ill newborns, or work exclusively with seriously ill newborns in a neonatal intensive care unit (NICU).

Minimum degree you'll need to practice: You must be a registered nurse with a Bachelor of Science in Nursing (BSN).

Certification: You must become certified by your State Board of Nursing or receive a national certification from an agency such as the National Certification Corporation.

Median annual salary: RN: $68,450*, NNP: $107,460*

Neonatal nurses (RNs) and neonatal nurse practitioners (NNPs) may work in clinics, community-based settings, hospitals or neonatal intensive care units. They may also conduct research, act as consultants or provide education to staff and family members. This nursing career requires a high level of diligence and teamwork. You will work closely with parents, neonatologists and other nurse specialists to achieve optimal results for your tiny patients.

There are three levels in the neonatal nursing specialty:

- Level I care for healthy infants. The demand for this level of neonatal nursing is decreasing because mothers and newborn babies are now more likely to stay in the same room together after birth.

- Level II nurses are much more in demand because premature and sick babies need constant attention.

- Level III nurses have the most intensive responsibilities, working in the NICU and monitoring seriously ill or premature infants around the clock. They check ventilators and incubators, make sure babies are responding well, and teach parents to care for their infants properly.

Entry-level requirements vary by location. At a minimum, you need to meet these requirements:

- A neonatal nurse must be a registered nurse (RN) with a four-year Bachelor of Science in Nursing Degree (BSN).

- You must be certified in Neonatal Resuscitation and/or Neonatal Intensive Care Nursing.

- You may also be required to complete a minimum number of years of clinical experience in a hospital setting.

- To become a neonatal nurse practitioner (NNP), you will also need a Master of Science in Nursing (MSN) degree. Many neonatal nursing schools offer this degree through a two-year Advanced Practice Neonatal Nursing (APNN) program. This type of program will prepare you for nursing licensure as a nurse practitioner (NP) and/or clinical nurse specialist (CNS).

d) palliative Care Hospice and palliative care nurses help ease the symptoms and suffering of patients who have progressive, terminal illnesses. Because they work to meet the psychological, spiritual, and social needs of patients and patients' families during their most difficult hours, hospice nurses are called upon to provide compassionate emotional support through end-of-life decisions, with sensitivity to a patient's cultural and religious values.

Hospice care provides support and comfort to dying patients and their families, often in the patient's home, but also in hospitals, hospice centers, nursing homes, and other long-term care facilities. According to the publication, Nurses for a Healthier Tomorrow, hospice care is often referred to as end-of-life care, as most hospice patients die within a month of enrolling into a hospice program.

Palliative care brings the principles of hospice care to people at an earlier stage of their illness. According to the National Hospice and Palliative Care Organization, palliative care effectively becomes hospice care as a person's illness progresses and death becomes inevitable.

Advanced Practice Hospice/Palliative Care Education

Many advanced practice nursing programs offer palliative care as a subspecialty, within a particular patient population. Specific MSN options include:

- Adult-Gerontology Primary Care Nurse Practitioner Specializing in Palliative Care

- Adult Nurse Practitioner/Palliative Care Nurse Practitioner

- Acute Care Nurse Practitioner with Hospice and Palliative Care Specialties
- Advanced Practice Adult Oncology/Palliative Care

Other options may be available. For example, some nursing schools lets students create a palliative care subspecialty by adding credits to the Family NP, Adult-Gerontological Acute Care NP, Adult-Gerontological Primary Care NP, or Clinical Nurse Specialist-Adult Health program. Other schools offer both palliative care and pediatric palliative care as distinct clinical specialties in MSN programs designed to qualify both NPs and CNSs.

Post-master's programs in palliative care are also available for advanced practice nurses who already have an MSN, and some DNP programs offer a palliative care subspecialty.

Advanced Practice Certification

The National Board for Certification of Hospice and Palliative Nurses (NBCHPN) offers specialty certification for all levels of hospice/palliative care nursing.

Both CNSs and NPs can take the Advanced Certified Hospice and Palliative Nurse (ACHPN) exam. In addition to having an active, current RN license in the United States or a comparable license in Canada, candidates must also have post-baccalaureate education through a program that meets one of the following criteria:

- Master's or higher in nursing from an advanced practice palliative care program that included both classroom training and at least 500 hours of supervised clinical practice in palliative care

- Post-master's certificate that included supervised clinical practice of at least 500 hours in palliative care

- Master's, post-master's or higher degree in nursing from an advanced practice program as a CNS or NP, plus post-master's practice of at least 500 hours in providing palliative care during the year before taking the certification exam

The exam has 175 questions covering five areas of practice related to the care of adult patients (age 12 and up) and their families:

- Clinical judgment
- Advocacy and ethics & systems thinking
- Professionalism and research
- Collaboration, facilitation of learning, and communication

Other books by:

Christine N. Malone

Addictions Through The Eyes of a Nurse, Rising Above Adversity Through Faith

&

The Fallen Woman, Becoming God's Best

www.ingramcontent.com/pod-product-compliance
Lightning Source LLC
LaVergne TN
LVHW021405080426
835508LV00020B/2470